STAR ON THE DOOR

A New Comedy
by
Jack Sharkey and Leo W. Sears

D1789370

SAMUEL FRENCH, INC.

45 WEST 25TH STREET   NEW YORK 10010
7623 SUNSET BOULEVARD   HOLLYWOOD 90046
LONDON   *TORONTO*

This play is fondly dedicated
to those two hot babes
JAN and PAT
who let
Leo and Jack
play together

IMPORTANT BILLING AND CREDIT REQUIREMENTS

All producers of STAR ON THE DOOR *must* give credit to the Authors of the Play in all programs distributed in connection with performances of the Play and in all instances in which the title of the Play appears for purposes of advertising, publicizing or otherwise exploiting the Play and/or a production. The names of the Authors *must* also appear on a separate line, on which no other name appears, immediately following the title, and *must* appear in size of type not less than fifty percent the size of the title type.

.

CHARACTERS
(in order of appearance)

BEVERLY — Doreen's personal assistant, attractive, 28.

MEL THORN — The producer of *The Inspector and the Aunt,* short, balding, 55.

DOREEN LEWIS — Eccentric, flamboyant actress, looks younger than her age, 60.

THOMAS — Doreen's son, handsome, 35.

PAUL BURNSIDE — Doreen's volatile leading man, 57.

WOLFGANG FERRIS — The hot-tempered Bavarian playwright of *The Inspector and the Aunt,* 40.

SETTING

The entire play takes place in the dressing room of Doreen Lewis the opening night of *The Inspector and the Aunt.*

ACT I
Doreen's dressing room, just before the curtain.

ACT II, SCENE 1
Doreen's dressing room, a few minutes before intermission.

ACT II, SCENE 1
Doreen's dressing room, about half an hour later.

(if necessary, play may be performed in Three Act format)

ACT I

*It is one hour before the curtain of the opening night
performance of the play* The Inspector and The Aunt.
*The painted-pink dressing room of Doreen Lewis. On
left wall, upstage is main entrance, downstage just
inches above floor is a framed picture of Lassie. On the
floor in front of the picture is a placemat with pet water
and food bowls. On right wall downstage is Doreen's
make-up mirror, table and chair. Above it is a clothes
rack. In center of room is loveseat, at slight angle
facing make-up table. On back wall are two terrible-
looking portraits of Doreen. One of the portraits looks
like it was painted by a six-year-old; the other is so
abstract that it could be a building* or *Doreen. Between
pictures is Doreen's costume rack. The room is covered
with terrible-looking plastic plants, except for one real
bouquet on upstage side of make-up table. As curtain
opens, BEVERLY is taping obviously old and worn
telegrams on the edge of the mirror. There is a KNOCK
at the main door.*

BEVERLY. Come in.

MEL. (*Dressed in tuxedo, enters; as soon as he has
taken a few steps inside door he takes in the room and
reacts.*) Yup. It's pink all right. You know, I had to have
this room painted twice. Doreen didn't like the first pink.
Said it was too much like *strawberry* ice cream. Said she
hates strawberry ice cream. It had to be bright—but not too

bright. So I got raspberry. Felt good, giving Doreen the *raspberry.*

BEVERLY. *(Continuing to tape up telegrams.)* You get used to it after awhile. Doreen *always* has her dressing room painted pink.

MEL. Reminds me of a *bordello*—or the bedroom of one of those romance novelists.

BEVERLY. You do get around, don't you!

MEL. *(Mirthlessly.)* Ho-ho. *(Walks to upstage wall and studies paintings.)* I know about her acting ability, but she certainly has atrocious taste in art. *(Looking at picture which appears to have been painted by a child.)* This painted by a *kid* she knows?

BEVERLY. *(Glancing back.)* That's a *self* portrait.

MEL. By *Doreen*?

BEVERLY. Who else?

MEL. Oh. *(Now looks at other.)* Where's *this* building?

BEVERLY. *(Begins to dust plants.)* That's another self-portrait.

MEL. I thought it was the Chrysler building.

BEVERLY. Doreen is quite proud of those paintings. Never had a lesson.

MEL. It shows.

BEVERLY. She's really an extraordinary lady.

MEL. So was Ma Barker. *(Looks at watch.)* Shouldn't she be here soon?

BEVERLY. She'll be here by seven, just like she's supposed to be. She hasn't missed a performance in her entire career. Don't worry.

MEL. I get paid to worry. You look up worry in the dictionary and it says "see producer." Investors don't like a flop. *(Looks at watch again.)* Where the hell is she?

BEVERLY. Mr. Thorn, *relax*! Doreen is always on time.

MEL. I *can't* relax. My knees keep anticipating machine-gun bullets!

BEVERLY. So *why* did you go to the mob for backing?

MEL. They contacted me. Some guy named *Nunzio*. Actually, I've never met *him* in person. The whole deal was put together through his attorney.

BEVERLY. Nunzio sounds like someone trying to support the arts.

MEL. He sounds like a charter member of the National Machine Gun Association.

BEVERLY. It's probably just your imagination.

MEL. (*Looks at his legs.*) I just don't want to look like Talouse Lautrec. I see my flowers arrived.

BEVERLY. They're lovely. She doesn't get many *real* flowers anymore. So she makes do with these. (*Indicates plastic flowers.*) *And* ten-year-old telegrams! Her dressing rooms used to be filled with telegrams and flowers. Her flowers would put many funerals to shame.

MEL. (*Looks at legs.*) Don't mention *funerals*!

DOREEN (*Suddenly DOREEN enters the room with THOMAS; she is carrying a stuffed toy dog; her dress is very bright, almost outlandish in its appearance.*) Good evening, Melvin. (*Hands toy dog to THOMAS.*) Please put Fluffy down by her bowl. (*THOMAS takes toy dog and sets it down on placemat.*) That (*Points to picture of Lassie.*) is Fluffy's favorite actor. She loves Lassie. Lassie sent Fluffy that autographed picture herself. The *bigger* they are! (*MEL is taken aback by all this, but BEVERLY and THOMAS don't react at all.*) I know you have a rule against animals backstage, but I'm sure you can bend the rules for *me*. Right, Melvin?

MEL. (*Almost dumbfounded.*) I'm sure—uh—? (*Looks at dog.*)

THOMAS. (*Helpfully.*) *Fluffy.*

MEL. —won't be a problem.

DOREEN. That's what I told Tony at the stage door. I like him, Melvin. (*Suddenly changes gears.*) Isn't tonight *exciting*? An opening night still thrills me. There's something about the challenge of that opening night audience and the critics. Even with all the opening nights I've had, the adrenalin still pumps. My *audience* still loves me. (*Looks around.*) Look at all these flowers—*and* the telegrams. It's *so* wonderful to be so loved by my public. Melvin, *what* happened to the interviews? You were supposed to have had them set up for this afternoon. I waited *all* afternoon for them. I even missed my nap.

THOMAS. (*Saving MEL.*) Mother, they probably didn't want to disturb your *preparation*. They know how important an *opening night* is to you.

MEL. (*Relieved.*) That's it. They didn't want to interfere with your preparation. The reporters wouldn't want to bother such a *professional*. I'm sure there will be plenty of reporters beating down your doors in the next few days. You won't be able to get any rest.

DOREEN. You're probably right. I'm certain that I shall be *buried* by reporters.

MEL. Don't say *"buried."*

DOREEN. How's that?

MEL. Never mind. You'll be *engulfed* by reporters. I'm sure of it.

DOREEN. You know my public just can't get enough of me. I once did a command performance at the White House. Harry played the piano adequately—but the man was *so* vulgar. Had a mouth like a sailor. I told Bess that until she got her husband's language under control I would never perform there again. But she never did, so *I* never did. The leader of the nation should set an example. I simply won't tolerate filthy language. I won't act in a play that has nasty language.

MEL. Doreen, we've *cut* all offensive language out of this play.

DOREEN. That *vile* Mister Williams—bless his soul—asked me to do one of his plays—

MEL. *Tennessee* Williams?

DOREEN. Of course, Melvin. But I simply couldn't convince the man to clean up his plays. I mean, I, Doreen Lewis, star of the silver screen, could not *afford* to be associated with some of the *smut* that man wrote.

MEL. You turned down Tennessee Williams?! I didn't think he *wrote* smut—?

DOREEN. Why, Blanche DuBois was a postbellum prostitute!

MEL. (*Even more incredulous.*) *You* turned down *Blanche Dubois*?!

THOMAS. Mother was just citing an example. Actually, she turned down Amanda Wingfield.

MEL. But *she* wasn't a prostitute!

BEVERLY. No, but she was old enough to be somebody's *mother*.

DOREEN. And I *wasn't*—at least not *then*. Even today, who'd believe I had a full-grown son! (*Smiles radiantly and squeezes Thomas's hand.*)

THOMAS. Mother, it's been in *all* the columns.

DOREEN. (*Shrugs off the idea.*) Bah, who believes what goes into the *columns!*

BEVERLY. They printed your *age* once.

DOREEN. And I never let them forget it!

THOMAS. They didn't *want* to forget it, Mother.

BEVERLY. And they update it every year.

DOREEN. I *hate* gossip columnists! (*Moves toward door.*) I'm going to check the set. (*Exits.*)

MEL. (*Calls after her.*) Check it for *what?*

THOMAS. That's just Mom's excuse when the conversation gets uncomfortable. She'll walk around the stage for five minutes saying, "Lovely, lovely!", and then come back, figuring we must have changed the subject.

MEL. (*Uneasily.*) What does she do if things get uncomfortable on the *set?*

BEVERLY. Don't ask.

MEL. (*Hand to stomach.*) Excuse me, I have to find my Maalox! (*Exits.*)

BEVERLY. Tommy—

THOMAS. Bev—

(They go into brief but torrid clinch-and-kiss; then;)

BEVERLY. Do you think she suspects?

THOMAS. Not yet. She's been so preoccupied learning her lines. Acting on stage isn't like the movies. You can't stop and go back for re-takes.

BEVERLY. Darling—no reflection on your *mother,* you understand, but—with the threat of mob vengeance hanging over his head—or pointing at his knees, anyhow—*why* in the world did Mel Thorn pick *her* to be in this play?

THOMAS. Bev, Mom's a *wonderful* actress!

BEVERLY. I know she is. In the *movies*. But this is *live*, Tommy. She drops lines, misses cues, and the *prompter* is about to ask for hazardous duty pay!

THOMAS. The part doesn't have *that* many lines. Mom's onstage a lot, but most of it is reaction stuff— facial stuff—fear, uncertainty, anger, unhappiness, like that. Mostly she tries not to be upstaged by Paul Burnside.

BEVERLY. He *does* tend to hog attention, all right!

THOMAS. He backed so far upstage during his first big speech, so Mom'd have to turn her back to the audience to keep him in sight, I thought he was going to back right up through the wall!

BEVERLY. But Doreen didn't let him get *away* with it, did she? No audience could possibly look at anyone on stage but *her*!

THOMAS. That's true, but Burnside got *awfully* steamed when he found out she'd tucked the rear hem of her gown into her bloomers!

BEVERLY. At least it happened out-of-town, and not here in New York. If *only* that news photographer hadn't been in the audience that night!

THOMAS. Remember the *caption* on the photo in the morning paper? *I'll* never forget it!

BEVERLY. Could anyone? There was suave old Burnside gabbing away, and there was your mom's rear in full view, and underneath the photo it said "The Man and the Moon"!

THOMAS. Mom *loved* it.

BEVERLY. Burnside didn't! He said if that was the kind of thing she liked to pull, he'd make his entrance with his *fly* unzipped!

THOMAS. Oh never mind about them—what about *us*? When are we going to tell Mom—

BEVERLY. Certainly *not* on Opening Night! Maybe later. When we've seen the reviews. If they're *good* reviews. After the show's been *running* a year—

THOMAS. A year? We've got less than nine months—and she's *sure* to notice before then.

BEVERLY. We're getting off the subject.

THOMAS. We are?

BEVERLY. You *still* haven't told me why Mel picked *Doreen* to save his knees from destruction!

THOMAS. I have a theory on that—I overheard Mel talking to Nunzio's attorney awhile back, and got the distinct impression that this Nunzio's a big *fan* of Mom's.

BEVERLY. You don't mean Mel was *forced* to use her?! Oh, Tommy, she'd *die* if she found out.

THOMAS. (*Shrugs.*) So who's going to *tell* her? *We* wouldn't—and Mel wouldn't *dare*. Mom's got a mean stranglehold, and the sharpest fingernails—!

BEVERLY. Well—

THOMAS. (*Takes her chin in one hand, gently kissing her on the lips.*) Relax. It'll all be fine.

BEVERLY. But for how long? I can't *keep* on pretending my morning-sickness is food-poisoning!

THOMAS. We'll *tell* her, we'll *tell* her! I just don't think Opening Night on Broadway is the perfect moment to tell an age-conscious woman she's soon to be a *grandmother*!

(BOTH look up as MEL re-enters, with something wrapped in tissue paper.)

MEL. Is Doreen *still* checking the set?!

BEVERLY. Well, it's got a lot of furniture—

THOMAS. What's in the paper?

MEL. *(Fussily unwrapping item.)* A last-ditch stand. You know your mother has *refused* to go on tonight until I put a *star* on her dressing-room door! I've looked *everywhere* for one. They don't seem to *make* them anymore!

BEVERLY. *(As MEL almost completes unwrapping.)* But you *found* one—?

MEL. Sort of. *(Holds up six-inch Star of David; they react; after a pause:)* I only hope she can't count.

THOMAS. Maybe if we painted the *bottom* point to match the *door*—

BEVERLY. But, Mel—if it's not *gold*—she'll *insist* on gold!

THOMAS. You'd better take it back.

MEL. Are you crazy? I'm sure that Bar Mitzvah's been over for *hours*—and that mob looked *mean*!

BEVERLY. *(Taking star.)* Here, give it to me. She's never been on Broadway before. I'll tell her it's a New York City tradition!

MEL. I don't want to be here when you do.

THOMAS. You won't be. You'll be out looking for gold paint!

MEL. *(Realizes.)* Right! *(Bolts from room fast.)*

BEVERLY. Does he have time to go shopping before the curtain goes up?

THOMAS. The farther he gets from the theater, the happier he'll be.

(BOTH react guiltily and move slightly apart as DOREEN rushes back into the room.)

DOREEN. I can't remember my opening line!

BEVERLY. (*Dryly.*) What else is new?

DOREEN. (*Has lurched to script on dressing table, is paging frantically through it.*) I know Paul's in the living room, as the police inspector, and the maid has left, and then I come into the room—but what do I *say*—?! (*Pages briefly, stops, reads, sighs in relief, closes script, turns to face them.*) Oh, of course!

THOMAS. What *is* your line?

DOREEN. "Good morning, Inspector."

BEVERLY. A real toughie.

THOMAS. Mother, it'll be fine once you actually get onstage, I know it will. *You* always remember what to say once you get into *character*.

DOREEN. That's true. I *do*, don't I. It's just that every time that lousy Paul Burnside pulls one of his tricks, I get *mad*, and *forget* to stay in character, and all at once I can't remember a *word* of this silly aunt's dialogue!

BEVERLY. If you hate him so much, why did you agree to Mel *selecting* him for the role?

DOREEN. Before we did *Murder, M'Lady?*, I didn't *know* Paul. Oh, I knew his *work*, and much admired him. It was only when I had to work with him that I discovered that *louse* lurking under all the pancake make-up and augmented hair! Melvin had asked me about *The Inspector's Aunt* when *Murder, M'Lady?* began. I said I'd do it—and *despite* my feelings regarding Paul, I *keep* my promises.

THOMAS. It'll be curtain time soon. You'd better get into costume, then get into character, and *stay* in character, and forget all about Paul Burnside!

DOREEN. It would take a miracle, Thomas. How could *anybody* forget such a cruel, selfish, ruthless, double-dealing, scene-stealing, no-good, bad-tempered—(*PAUL BURNSIDE steps into dressing-room at this moment, and she switches without even a fractional hesitation to full-kilowatt charm, not even pausing for breath as she continues:*) Paul, *darling*, it's so good to see you! (*Rushes to give him a hug and kiss.*)

PAUL. (*With syrupy charm.*) Doreen, how *wonderful* to see you again! (*Breaks obligatory hug.*) I just couldn't imagine us working onstage together again—so soon. I'm sorry we didn't have much of a chance to chat during rehearsals, but *you* know how busy we were. If we weren't blocking, then we were each learning our lines. How long has it been since our first play together, Doreen?

DOREEN. I'm not sure. (*Turns to BEVERLY.*) Beverly, dear, how long has it been? (*Back to PAUL.*) I just keep *so* busy that I have no idea of the time. It just flies by.

BEVERLY. You and Mister Burnside first worked together on that mystery *Murder, M'Lady?* That would have been some two-and-a-half years ago.

PAUL. Amazing. It seems just like yesterday. A shame it folded out of town.

DOREEN. Yes. How could I forget that play?

PAUL. (*To himself.*) God knows how hard I've tried.

DOREEN. Beg pardon?

PAUL. It fills my heart with pride!

DOREEN. Mine too! That exhilarating return to the stage after so many years of just film work. Once you learn you never forget. Like riding a bicycle.

PAUL. (*To himself.*) That's what you looked like, all right.

DOREEN. How's that?

PAUL. You looked all right!—got your lines down solid?

DOREEN. (*Very indignant.*) I am a *professional.* I'm insulted that you could even mention such a thing. Doreen Lewis always has her lines memorized and prepared. If people would just stop giving me the wrong cues. I always have my lines. Always. Always. I think I'll go check the set. (*Exits.*)

PAUL. That crazy old lady *better* know her lines!

THOMAS. (*Coming to DOREEN's defense.*) Don't worry, Mother will be fine.

PAUL. She scares me to death. In *Murder, M'Lady?* she came onstage after she'd been murdered. She overacts. And I still haven't forgotten her gown tucked into her bloomers.

THOMAS. I'm sure that was accidental, Paul.

BEVERLY. I should have noticed it before she went onstage.

PAUL. That woman has far too many problems onstage.

THOMAS. The only reason Mother has problems onstage is that you seem to rattle her. She's sure you're always trying to upstage her.

PAUL. Me? Upstage? Never!—Except in self-defense. Otherwise Doreen would steal every scene.

THOMAS. But I think it's your defensiveness that gets her rattled!

PAUL. A pity she doesn't rattle *out loud.* Then I'd know when she's about to strike!

BEVERLY. If you hate sharing the stage with Doreen, why ever did you agree to be in this play?

PAUL. Mel talked me into it. He says that one of the investors is a big fan of her movies. Frankly, so am I, and Mel knew that when he started coaxing. (*Drifts off.*) Who could forget her early films? She was so gorgeous, so sensitive, talented, breathtakingly beautiful—(*Back to reality.*) Anyway, I let Mel convince me. It didn't take much convincing. I must be crazy. (*Notices "other performer" onstage, reacts, points.*) What—is—that?!

BEVERLY. You mean Fluffy?

PAUL. Achoo! What in the world is that dog doing backstage? Achoo! Doreen knows better than that! It's against the health laws! Achoo! And she knows I'm *allergic* to animal dander! She—achoo—did this on purpose! She's trying to destroy me! When I tell Mel—!

THOMAS. Mel knows all about Fluffy. What you don't realize is that—

PAUL. Equity's going to hear about this! I'm filing a formal complaint. Achoo! Either that dog goes, or I go!

BEVERLY. Paul, your allergic reaction is totally psychosomatic!

THOMAS. It's all in your head!

PAUL. That's because my *nose* is in my head! Achoo! (*Starts doorward.*) I've got to get out of here!

THOMAS. Paul, you're just imagining things!

PAUL. Achoo! That sneeze was not imaginary!

BEVERLY. Just unnecessary.

PAUL. What are you talking about?

THOMAS. (*Picking up Fluffy.*) This dog is made of synthetic fibers. It's stuffed.

BEVERLY. So your nose shouldn't be.

PAUL. Synthetic fi—? (*Peers closely at toy.*) I'll be damned. It looked so real!

THOMAS. (*Replacing Fluffy on floor.*) Only the best for Doreen Lewis.

PAUL. (*Has been using handkerchief, now replaces it.*) Is that woman crazy or what?

BEVERLY. Not as crazy as your nose! I mean, Paul, you have nothing to sneeze about, but look at you!

PAUL. You're right. My analyst will never believe this. I'm sane, but my nose is crazy!

BEVERLY. Not *that* crazy, Paul. The creature certainly looks real. It would fool *anybody's* nose!

PAUL. But why does Doreen even have a *stuffed* dog?

THOMAS. It looks just like her real dog Fluffy who died a few months ago.

PAUL. She'd had Fluffy fifteen years.

THOMAS. The toy substitute kind of eases the loss.

PAUL. Say no more. I understand everything. Well, *almost* everything.

BEVERLY. Meaning what?

PAUL. Why are you toting that Star of David? Or are we doing a benefit for B'nai Brith?

BEVERLY. Oh, this? I forgot I was holding it. (*Sets it on dressing table.*)

PAUL. But why were you holding it at all?

THOMAS. We figured that Mel would be back any moment with the gold paint.

PAUL. If you think that clears matters up—! Oh, never mind. (*Looks at wristwatch.*) I've got to get ready. I hope for our sakes that Doreen doesn't screw up tonight! (*Exits.*)

THOMAS. Can you believe that guy? From the way he feels about performing with my mother, Mel must've gotten him *drunk* to sign that contract.

BEVERLY. (*Casually checking belly-profile at mirror.*) Men! You're so blind! You never notice *anything*!

THOMAS. (*Patiently amused.*) Bev, there's nothing to notice *yet*! Maybe in three or four months—

BEVERLY. (*Faces him.*) I was *not* referring to my pregnancy, Tom!

THOMAS. (*At sea.*) Then what *didn't* I notice that got your *dander* up?

BEVERLY. (*Pulls him slightly away from open door.*) Ssh! Don't mention dander where Paul might hear you! Just *thinking* about his allergy sets it off!

THOMAS. Yeah, any guy who'd react to a stuffed Fluffy—

BEVERLY. He was not reacting to *Fluffy*! Don't you understand *anything*?!

THOMAS. Hey, easy, girl! I heard pregnant women get emotional, but what did *I* do to upset you?

BEVERLY. (*Arms akimbo.*) You *got* me pregnant! How's that for *starters*?!

THOMAS. (*Calmly.*) Correction. *We* got you pregnant. You were there *too*, remember?

BEVERLY. (*Softens.*) Do I ever! (*Slips comfortably into his arms.*) It was *such* a lovely wedding night!

THOMAS. (*This time he pulls her away from door.*) Ssh! Not so loud! If Mom finds out we ran off and got married without inviting *her*—

BEVERLY. How *could* we? She was back in Monaco, doing voice-looping for that killer-contessa movie! Has your mother appeared in *anything* on stage or screen that didn't involve murder? When does that come out, anyhow? I hope it's in time for the Oscar nominations—

THOMAS. Whoa! We're getting *way* off the subject!

BEVERLY. I thought the subject was our marriage, which we managed to pull off because for the first time in seven years your mother didn't need *me* doing the slave-labor as her *dresser*!

THOMAS. *Forget* our marriage!

BEVERLY. (*Mock-wistfully.*) You've tired of me so *soon*? (*Half-turns away, but—*)

THOMAS. (*He pulls her back to face him.*) I mean forget it as conversation fodder. I want to get to that *earlier* crack, when you said my getting you pregnant for "starters"! What are you so upset about about *tonight*?

BEVERLY. You really don't know, do you? Men are *so* stupid! (*Pushes him away.*) You especially.

THOMAS. Stupid about *what*?

BEVERLY. Paul and Doreen!

THOMAS. What *about* Paul and Doreen?

BEVERLY. They're in *love,* you idiot!

THOMAS. (*Stares at her, gape-jawed, for about two seconds; then:*) With *each other*?!

BEVERLY. Of *course* with each other.

THOMAS. But—those things she said—the way he sneezed—? They sure don't *act* like lovers!

BEVERLY. They don't *know* they're in love, you imbecile!

THOMAS. Now, hold on! They're in *love,* but they don't *know* they're in love, so *I'm* an imbecile?!

BEVERLY. That pretty much sums things up.

THOMAS. The *hell* it does!

BEVERLY. Look, Doreen keeps going out to the check the set because she can't *trust* herself when he's near!

THOMAS. And Paul's psychosomatic sneezing—?

BEVERLY. He feels *betrayed* she'd bring an *animal* near his *allergies*!

THOMAS. Then they *do* know they care. They must!

BEVERLY. Why?

THOMAS. A man *can't* feel betrayed by an enemy, and a woman *can* trust herself when a *schlemiel* is near!

BEVERLY. But, darling, they don't *recognize* the reasons for the churned-up emotions.

THOMAS. And you *do*?

BEVERLY. Of course! A disinterested observer *always* notices things like that. *My* emotions aren't clouding my *reason*!

THOMAS. I thought you *liked* Mom.

BEVERLY. Who says I *don't*?

THOMAS. If you have no *interest* in her problem—

BEVERLY. Tommy, I said I was *dis*interested, not *un*interested! There's a big difference.

THOMAS. What difference?

BEVERLY. Plenty!

THOMAS. You call that an explanation?

BEVERLY. It's more than you deserve!

THOMAS. Then you *are* mad at me!

BEVERLY. Don't be ridiculous! (*Goes into his arms.*) I *love* you, you birdbrain! (*Kisses him good.*)

THOMAS. (*When their lips unmesh.*) Let's be logical for a minute. You say I'm a birdbrain—?

BEVERLY. Right.

THOMAS. But you're in *love* with me—?

BEVERLY. Even righter.

THOMAS. Then—doesn't that make *you* even *more* of a birdbrain?

BEVERLY. (*Sighs, pillows her cheek against his chest.*) Probably.

THOMAS. (*Pillows his cheek atop her head.*) So we're *both* nuts.

BEVERLY. But mostly about each other.

THOMAS. Ain't it the truth! (*They kiss again; then:*)

BEVERLY. (*Disengages from him.*) I *wish* the lab report would come!

THOMAS. Bev, are you telling me you're not *sure* you're pregnant?

BEVERLY. (*Moves to mirror, profile-checks belly again.*) Oh, sure I am. Deep down inside. It's a kind of—*glow.* A physical sensation of—oh—*motherliness.* I just—well—*feel* pregnant.

THOMAS. Yeah, but what if it turns out that you merely—um—*miscounted* or something?

BEVERLY. Tommy, I've *never* been *this* late before. A couple of *days,* maybe—certainly not *three weeks*! And then, of course, there's the *morning* sickness—

THOMAS. Which could be as psychosomatic as Fluffy's dander! You could be *thinking* yourself pregnant!

BEVERLY. (*Turns her back to him, asks wistfully:*) And would—would that—make you *happy,* Tommy —?

THOMAS. (*Firmly turns to her to face him, hands on her shoulders.*) What, and lose this physical sensation of—oh—*fatherliness*? (*She laughs; he mimics her:*) It's a kind of—*glow*!

BEVERLY. You lunatic! (*They almost clinch again, but she back-steps abruptly, on:*) Cool it! I think I hear Doreen coming back! (*He turns to study telegram on mirror, she pretends to be adjusting a bottle or jar on make-up table, and DOREEN enters, looking distraught.*)

THOMAS. Oh, hi there! Set check out okay?

DOREEN. (*Fingertips going briefly to her temples.*) I suppose so—I have other things to worry about. Is *Mel* throwing an opening-night party after the show—or am I? Or is *anybody*?

BEVERLY. (*Soothingly.*) When the curtain falls—always assuming you and Paul haven't murdered one another during the play—we all trot merrily out of Shubert Alley and reconvene at—

DOREEN. The Stork Club! Of course! How *could* I have forgotten?!

THOMAS. Uh, Mother—the Stork Club's been out of business for years—

DOREEN. (*Quick fluster-and-recovery and into:*) Oh how silly of me! I meant Toots Shor's, of course! I always mix them up because they both have the "*or*"-sound.

BEVERLY. Uh, Doreen—

DOREEN. No Toots?

BEVERLY. No Toots. Since more than a decade.

DOREEN. Then *where* in the world—?

THOMAS. Sardi's. And Mel is playing host.

DOREEN. Now, wait, you can't be right. I distinctly remember Sardi's shut down—

BEVERLY. They re-opened.

DOREEN. Oh, dear. I wonder if I'm getting senile.

THOMAS. Impossible.

DOREEN. I don't see *why*.

THOMAS. Because you're female, for one thing. *Men* get senile; women get *anile*.

DOREEN. I hope you don't think that cheers me up? I keep forgetting *so* many things—

THOMAS. Mother, you are not having memory-lapses. You're just trying to think of too many things at once. Your lines, your blocking, your—um—?

DOREEN. Yes—?

THOMAS. Oh—*lots* of things!

BEVERLY. Say, maybe *you're* getting senile!

THOMAS. (*Defensively.*) I have enough things of my *own* to remember, without keeping tabs on all of *Mother's* mental-storage items!

DOREEN. But why *do* I forget so many things, more and more of them, lately? I used to be so great with *names*—people I'd meet just once, and five years later I'd call them by name—

BEVERLY. Calm down, Doreen. It's your *age* that's the problem, but—

DOREEN. You think I *am* getting—what did you call it—*anile*, then?

BEVERLY. Not even slightly.

THOMAS. Then what did you mean about her *age*?

BEVERLY. Do you realize how many *encounters* Doreen has made in her life? A newborn only has to know "Mama" and "Dada"; with a career like Doreen's, meeting literally *thousands* of new people every year, it's no *wonder* a few things slip through the cracks.

DOREEN. Then you think it's perfectly natural—not an advance warning of mental decrepitude?

THOMAS. Of course it's natural. Bev's right. By your age, there are just too *many* things to keep in mind. So you simply shuck off the surplus, and hang onto the important stuff.

DOREEN. Well—I *do* hope you're right.

BEVERLY. Of course he's right. Now just sit down at the dressing table and start getting into make-up. That *always* relaxes you. Something about the soothing smell of the grease paint, you've always said.

DOREEN. (*Stares blankly.*) I *have*? Then why don't I *remember* always having said that?

THOMAS. (*Whips up tube of grease paint, holds it under her nose.*) Here, smell!

DOREEN. (*Sniffs, then smiles, takes tube from him.*) It *is* a relaxing kind of odor, isn't it!

BEVERLY. So you always say! (*ALL laugh; then:*)

DOREEN. Now, shoo, Thomas, I've got to get into costume!

THOMAS. I didn't hear half-hour—?

DOREEN. I passed the call-boy onstage on my way back here. It's *past* half-hour!

THOMAS. Okay. Mom. I'm heading out front. (*Pecks DOREEN on cheek.*) Break a leg, Beautiful! (*He exits, shutting dressing room door behind him.*)

DOREEN. Where *did* I put my costume?!

BEVERLY. (*Moving to point upstage of screen.*) You didn't. I did. It's right here. (*Lifts lovely nightgown into view.*) See?

DOREEN. (*Moving up to join her behind screen.*) I make my first entrance in a *nightgown*?

BEVERLY. After the gunshots, remember?

(General business of DOREEN getting costumed, with now-and-then assist from BEVERLY.)

DOREEN. My line! My opening line! What do I say when—?

BEVERLY. It's morning right after the murder. The maid has told the inspector that the old double-barreled pistol over the mantel cannot *possibly* be the murder weapon because it's merely a decoration, and right after she leaves to summon you, the inspector takes the pistol to the French doors and tries firing it toward the garden, and—

DOREEN. Yes-yes, and it goes off, quite startling him, and then *I* enter, but what do I say?

BEVERLY. (*Amazed DOREEN can't remember:*) You say "Good morning, Inspector"!

DOREEN. Oh, of course, how silly of me. What *else* would I say!

BEVERLY. It'll all come back to you, all of it, the moment you step onstage. It always does.

(There is a KNOCK at the door.)

DOREEN. (*Agitated.*) Now, who would *dare* interrupt me when I'm getting ready for—?

(Door opens and PAUL, now in costume, peeks in.)

PAUL. Doreen—?

DOREEN. (*Nastily.*) I might have *known*! Honestly, Paul, this is *not* a good time for a chat!

BEVERLY. Why don't you wait outside, and the moment she's ready, I'll—

PAUL. (*Moves to chair and sits, politely keeping his back toward screen.*) Nonsense! Doreen's entrance is in her nightclothes! I've already seen *Doreen* in her nightclothes!

DOREEN. You've *what*—?! Oh, you mean dress rehearsal?

PAUL. Well, that, *too*, of course!

DOREEN. Paul Burnside, *what* are you implying?! And whatever he says is a *lie*, Beverly.

BEVERLY. Listen, perhaps I'd better *leave*—? (*Comes from behind screen about two steps.*)

PAUL. So I can compromise her *again*?

DOREEN. Paul, will you *stop* with those silly innuendoes!

PAUL. Of course. They're not what I've come to discuss *anyhow*!

DOREEN. Then what *have* you, of all the ill-timed moments, come to discuss?!

PAUL. That "morals clause" in my play-contract!

DOREEN. What about it? It's in *my* play-contract, too. It's in *all* the contracts. I had Mel put it in specially.

PAUL. But producers *never* put that clause in contracts any more, what with almost every other actress on Broadway having some co-star's child on the way these days.

BEVERLY. They'd have to shut down every other production if they enforced it.

PAUL. Bev, are you *still* here? (*Half-turns his head.*) I thought I said I wished to speak to Doreen in *private*?

BEVERLY. No, you didn't. But, as long as you *do*— excuse me. (*Starts for door.*)

DOREEN. Stay right outside the door. If I scream, telephone the police!

BEVERLY. And tell them what? (*Poises just short of exit, hand on doorknob.*)

PAUL. That Doreen Lewis is being irresistible again!

BEVERLY. That sounds fair enough. (*Exits, shutting door.*)

DOREEN. Now, *please*, Paul, get to the point and then get *out* of here! (*Comes from behind screen in nightgown, starts donning elegant frilly peignoir.*) Why shouldn't there be a morals clause in your contract? You're *moral*, aren't you?

PAUL. (*Stands and moves aside so she can sit and do last-minute facial makeup at table.*) If *you* don't know, *nobody* does!

DOREEN. What's *that* supposed to mean? Why do I feel I'm being *accused* of something sinister?

PAUL. Now, *don't* tell me you've *forgotten* what happened the night following the first rehearsal?

DOREEN. (*Stops for an infinitesimal moment, so we can see she has forgotten, but then she lies:*) Of *course* not! I—I never forget *anything*! It's part of an actress's basic training, quick memorization. But—that was four weeks ago—could you give me a *hint* what you're talking about?

PAUL. We were going to chat, remember? It had been so many years since we'd last worked together, back when your late husband was still on the scene. It was going to be an update of sorts.

DOREEN. (*Still lying:*) Oh, yes, of course. *Now* I remember. But what's that got to do with —?

PAUL. If you don't remember *everything* that happened that night, I'll quite understand.

DOREEN. (*Hesitates in her making-up, then continues, speaking casually.*) You—you *will*? Then I'm afraid *I* don't quite understand.

PAUL. Doreen, we didn't *have* our chat. Oh, we *initiated* it. You invited me up to your apartment, laid on the drinks with a lavish hand, and we *started* our trip down Memory Lane—

DOREEN. (*Very uneasily, applying makeup with increased diligence.*) *And*—?

PAUL. You got completely pie-eyed and passed out cold!

DOREEN. (*It's no use now; she ceases making-up, turns to face him.*) So *that's* it! You're threatening to *reveal* what I did, and then *invoke* that morals clause, *exposing* me as some sort of *alcoholic*?!

PAUL. (*Amazed.*) Exposing *you*? I thought *you* were going to use it to expose, *me*!

DOREEN. (*Reels, almost falling off her chair.*) Paul! You don't *mean*—while I was unconscious—?!

PAUL. (*Firmly.*) No, I *don't* mean! I did the gentlemanly thing, of course.

DOREEN. (*Hopefully.*) Tiptoed out and shut the door?

PAUL. There was no *need* to tiptoe. You wouldn't have heard an *elephant* stampede in your condition!

DOREEN. So—then—what exactly *did* you do?

PAUL. Put you to *bed*, of course! How do you think I got to see you in your *nightclothes*?

DOREEN. (*Comes to her feet.*) You *undressed* me? !

PAUL. You *were* undressed!

DOREEN. *What*?!

PAUL. I don't mean *naked*, Doreen. You got into your pajamas and robe *before* the drinks! Said your girdle was killing you and your shoes even worse, so you got *comfortable. Then* we had our drinks.

DOREEN. (*Sinks weakly back onto chair.*) Well, *that's* a relief! I—I suppose I should really have thanked you— but unfortunately didn't *remember* the event. Oh, Paul, you truly *are* a gentleman!

PAUL. Then you're *not* angry with me? When I saw the morals clause, I thought—

DOREEN. Say, just exactly when *did* you see that clause? The signing was more than two *months* ago.

PAUL. (*Guiltily.*) About ten minutes ago. I'd done my make-up and costume, I couldn't face looking at my *lines* one more time without *screaming,* but had a lot of time to kill, so—?

DOREEN. (*Laughs.*) Are you telling me that you, an intelligent adult male, signed that contract for Melvin without even *reading* it?

PAUL. Get real, Dorey-honey. In the precarious existence known as *acting,* one does *not,* when presented with the co-starring *lead* in a Broadway play, tell the producer, (*In very gruff and stuffy mock-up voice:*) "Well, now, not so fast, I have to read this thing very *carefully* first!"

DOREEN. One just lurches for the pen and says "Where do I sign?!" Yes, you're quite right. It *is* a precarious lifestyle, isn't it!

PAUL. (*Much relieved.*) So when I came across that *clause,* naturally, I really got the jimjams about it. Who knows what secret sin of mine might suddenly pop·up center stage in the splash of ten-thousand klieg lights?!

DOREEN. Well, then—(*Rises, takes his hand.*) Have I set your mind at ease, old friend?

PAUL. You truly have, kind lady. (*Bows gallantly, kisses her hand.*)

BEVERLY. (*Outside door, KNOCKS loudly, calls:*) Five minutes, you guys!

DOREEN. Whoops, where does the time go!

PAUL. See you onstage, babe.

DOREEN. Yes, "Inspector"!

(*PAUL laughs and exits out of the room as BEVERLY re-enters.*)

BEVERLY. My goodness, you two seemed almost *chummy*!

DOREEN. He—he *is* nice, isn't he!

BEVERLY. A lot of people seem to think so. Listen, if you don't need me for anything else, I'd like to join your son out front for the show.

DOREEN. Oh, of course, dear. Hurry off, now. See you later! (*BEVERLY exits, shutting door; DOREEN peers into mirror, does a final hair-fluff, gives a that's-about-as-good-as-I'll-ever-look shrug, and starts for the door; The PHONE RINGS; a bit bemused, she answers it, and says, on phone:*) Hello—?—Who?—Oh, yes, this *is* Mrs. Lewis—*What* lab report?—(*Listens and her eyes slowly widen with dismay, and then she shouts into the phone:*) I'm *WHAT*?!—But that's impossible!—I haven't—I mean—there's no *way* I could have—?! (*Stops; casts a sudden Dark Suspicion look toward the closed door; then, back into phone:*) How—how *long* have I been pregnant?—You don't say! (*A tight smile now contorts her face as she announces into telephone:*) Well, that's what I get for *chatting* with a *gentleman*! (*Hangs up phone with a*

slam.) That monster! That low, conniving, unscrupulous—
(*Yet another light dawns:*) The *morals* clause! So that's
what he's up to! Thinks he can get *me* kicked out of the
show, does he! Well, he'd better think again! (*Looks
around, as if for a weapon, sights in on something, rushes
to unseen area to get a luxurious fur stole; as she slips it
on, MEL comes rushing into room, carrying a can of gold
spray-paint, which he whips behind his back the moment
he sees her, nervously.*)

MEL. Doreen! I thought you'd be onstage!

DOREEN. Just going, Melvin dear. By the way,
remember the insurance physical all your players had to
take?

MEL. That's standard procedure for a Broadway show,
Doreen. What about it?

DOREEN. Well, I just heard the results from the
doctor!

MEL. On opening night?! Oh, my, I hope you're all
right—?

DOREEN. Healthy as a horse. No, make that a brood
mare! (*She starts to exit, but stops as MEL realizes:*)

MEL. Why are you wearing your mink? I mean wearing
it over your nightgown ?

DOREEN. I play a *very* wealthy woman in this show,
Melvin.

MEL. But—as I recall—isn't Paul Burnside *allergic* to
fur?

DOREEN. To *animal dander,* Melvin. There's no dander
on a *processed* fur, you know.

MEL. Yes, but does *Paul* know?

DOREEN. We're going to find *out,* aren't we! (*TWO
GUNSHOTS, off.*) Ah, there's my cue! (*Exits.*)

MEL. But, Doreen—!

DOREEN. (*Off, in dramatic loudness.*) "Good morning, Inspector—!" (*And we hear Paul's "ACHOO!"*)

CURTAIN
END OF ACT I

ACT II

Scene 1

Doreen's dressing room, a few minutes before intermission. The door is open. We hear PAUL sneeze, off, followed by a huge roar of AUDIENCE-LAUGHTER. THOMAS and BEVERLY enter, their faces decidedly unhappy.

THOMAS. My mother must be out of her mind. If she and Paul are in love, somebody ought to tell them! It's like watching a pair of half-starved lions circling the same lamb chop.

BEVERLY. If either of their careers survive this performance, it'll be a miracle. (*Starts arranging make-up-freshening items on dressing table.*)

THOMAS. If either of *them* survives, it'll be a miracle! It's a damn good thing that stage-gun is loaded with blanks!

BEVERLY. Maybe the show will fold fast, and no one will remember how awfully they behaved.

THOMAS. Are you kidding? Mel has stocked the theater with every influential showbiz person he knows and every newspaper critic in New York. The whole *world's* gonna know about them! Doreen's triumphal return to the theater is turning into her swan song! (*AUDIENCE-LAUGHTER off; he cringes.*) There's no way anyone out front is going to forget tonight! The night Paul Burnside and Doreen Lewis committed synchronized suicide onstage.

BEVERLY. We'd better hide anything that can be used as a weapon when they come off.

THOMAS. Why? Paul can take her out with his bare hands.

BEVERLY. Not while he's holding a box of Kleenex.

(PAUL-SNEEZE and AUDIENCE LAUGHTER off.)

THOMAS. And when it runs out?

BEVERLY. We could have a fight backstage that'd top a championship boxing match.

THOMAS. Maybe Mel could recoup his losses by selling tickets to it. "In this corner, wearing an allergy mask—!" *(Glances out door.)* Oh-oh, here comes Mel now! He doesn't look well.

BEVERLY. Mel *never* looks well.

THOMAS. Okay, he doesn't look *weller*!

BEVERLY. Is he armed? He may wipe those two out before they can wipe each other out!

THOMAS. And who could blame him?!

(MEL lurches in, almost staggering, his eyes a bit glazed.)

MEL. I'm ruined. The play's ruined. My *knees* are gonna be ruined! With every sneeze, I think, "Goodbye, Knees!"

(GUNSHOT off; MEL dives onto the floor.)

THOMAS. (*Business of helping MEL to his feet again.*) Relax, will you?

MEL. Why did I get into showbiz anyhow? I could have been happy as a bridge toll collector. Sure people spit at you and call you names, but at least your knees are protected!

BEVERLY. (*Finished at dressing table now.*) Mel, take it easy. Things could be worse.

MEL. Isn't that what they told Pharaoh just before the plagues? I'll bet this is how the captain of the Titanic felt. Except icy waters don't hurt your knees. They say death by drowning is almost pleasant!

THOMAS. How do they *know*? All the swollen blue faces are wearing *smiles*?

MEL. Whatever *possessed* your mother to wear that fur stole onstage with Paul? She *knew* what it would do! Paul sounds like he's auditioning for an Allerest commercial.

THOMAS. I'm as baffled as you are. But not as confused as Beverly! *She* thinks those two are in *love*!

BEVERLY. They are! I'm sure of it! They just haven't found out yet.

MEL. They'll be dead before they do. I've seen more warmth between the North and South Koreans!

THOMAS. Aw, Mel, it isn't *that* bad, is it?

MEL. You've got to be kidding! Every time Paul gets near Doreen, he sneezes. The blocking's gone out the window because she's chasing him around the stage. It's like watching a fuzzy bear chasing an asthmatic steam engine!

BEVERLY. The *audience* doesn't seem to mind.

MEL. Of course not! They think they're watching a Tom and Jerry cartoon! I thought it took years of practice to provoke laughter from the stage. All it takes is sneezing powder. The only nice thing about tonight is that the *playwright* isn't out front! Wolfgang Ferris has a violent temper. Thank heaven he's home in Austria. I don't know which would be worse, running into Nunzio's boys or running into Wolfgang. And there's no place to hide!

THOMAS. Aren't you overacting a little? People don't commit murder over terrible plays.

BEVERLY. If they did, the population of New York would be down to about three dozen people. (*Looks at wristwatch.*) Mel, it's almost time for intermission. You sure you want to be here when they come offstage?

MEL. I'm not worried about Doreen and Paul. The most they'll do is kill *each other*! Murder's habit-forming. They've murdered the show, they've murdered their careers, they may as well murder each other. Let them! I've got a pair of *knees* to protect! Excuse me! (*Bolts out of room.*)

THOMAS. Gosh, it's like watching a wounded tuna running away from a great white shark. Would this Nunzio person *really* blow his knees away?

BEVERLY. That or set his feet into a bucket of cement and go for a rowboat-ride on the East River. And I'll bet you ten dollars his little blue face would *not* be wearing a smile.

THOMAS. Let's hope and pray Nunzio isn't in the *audience* tonight!

BEVERLY. If *you* invested a small fortune in a show, where would *you* be tonight?

THOMAS. Maybe Nunzio's work schedule got in the way! A man like that is bound to be busy—heads to crack, contracts to get out, politicians to bribe, horseheads to put to bed—

BEVERLY. Stop! I get the point. Hey, I have to get Doreen's costume ready for the second act. (*Moves to clothes rack.*)

THOMAS. Will there *be* a second act?

BEVERLY. If we can keep Paul's hands off your mother's throat.

THOMAS. My worry is that he'll be nice as pie for the intermission, and then go back onstage with *real bullets* in that gun! I hope her *next* costume doesn't have fur on it, or the second act'll be sneeze-bang-thud!

BEVERLY. Sorry, but I don't see a bullet-proof vest on the rack. Don't worry, there's no fur on anything she's *supposed* to wear. Just get that stole away from her.

THOMAS. I'll try.

BEVERLY. You'd better. I'd like our child to have a grandmother for a *little* while at least!

THOMAS. (*Testing the words on his tongue.*) "Grandmother. Grandma Doreen." If words could kill, those'll do it. It's too much in one night, finding out she's a mother-in-law *and* a soon-to-be grandmother. She'll *die* when you tell her.

BEVERLY. *Me* tell her?! Hold the phone, chum! *You* were going to tell her!

THOMAS. I changed my mind.

BEVERLY. Can't the two of us tell her *together?*

THOMAS. Oh, all right. We will. While we're leaving. From our car. As we're driving off. We'll *yell* the good news. From about a block away. Two blocks away. Maybe we could phone her at home.

BEVERLY. Some heritage our kid will have: "Honey, your grandmother is a famous murder-victim and your father is a *chicken*!" (*GUNSHOT off.*) Hey, that's the final gunshot before the first-act curtain!

THOMAS. You've been *counting*?

BEVERLY. *Somebody* had to! (*APPLAUSE off.*) See? I told you it's the curtain. The audience is applauding.

THOMAS. Maybe they're just being appreciative that Paul hasn't strangled Doreen.

BEVERLY. Or that he *has*? (*Looks out doorway.*) Here she comes. Hold onto your hat.

DOREEN. (*Storms into room.*) Why didn't somebody tell me *Wolfgang Ferris* was out front? (*Much business of removing costume, adjusting make-up, etc., over upcoming speeches.*)

BEVERLY. He *is*? Poor Mel.

THOMAS. You *saw* him.

DOREEN. Of *course* I saw him! But even if I didn't, I'd know that whimper anywhere!

BEVERLY. You *would*?

DOREEN. How many Broadway first-nighters keep moaning "*Ach, himmel*!"?

THOMAS. Where's Paul? I thought he'd be charging in here after you with a fire axe!

DOREEN. Nope, he headed directly for his dressing room. It'll take him *most* of intermission to cover his rosey-red nose with make-up!

BEVERLY. How could you *do* such a thing to him, Doreen?

DOREEN. After what *he* did to *me*, my revenge is practically *petty*.

THOMAS. Mother, what *possibly* could Paul have *done* to you that makes destroying his *career* your crazed goal?

DOREEN. (*Seated, applying make-up, pauses, turns, takes him by hand.*) You know how you've always wanted a little brother or sister?

BEVERLY. Whoa! How did we suddenly change the subject?

DOREEN. We didn't, dear. Thomas, you're going to get your wish!

THOMAS. (*Knees buckle.*) What—?!

BEVERLY. Doreen, you don't mean—?

DOREEN. I wish I didn't!

THOMAS. Mother! What are you saying? I'm going to have a sibling?!

DOREEN. I only wish it *were* you who's going to have it! Unfortunately, basic biology has *other* ideas.

BEVERLY. But, Doreen—to have a child—at your age—it's so risky—?!

DOREEN. Damn it all, Beverly, I *hope* you don't think the little newcomer was *my* idea?!

THOMAS. Then whose *was* it?!

BEVERLY. (*The light begins to dawn.*) Oh, Doreen, you don't mean—?

THOMAS. (*Whose light is still out.*) *What*?

BEVERLY. So the explanation is simply that—

THOMAS. What?

DOREEN. (*Pats Beverly's hand.*) I'm so glad you understand.

THOMAS. *What*?

BEVERLY. (*To Doreen, but while looking with chagrin toward THOMAS.*) Men are *so* slow on the uptake!

THOMAS. Only because *women* never finish their sentences! *Who* the hell got you *pregnant*?

DOREEN. Darling, remember when I took you to see *Snow White*, which dwarf had the red nose?

(We hear PAUL SNEEZE, off.)

THOMAS. Paul? Paul Burnside? Do you mean he—do you mean he's the one who—the one that—

BEVERLY. (*Finishing for him.*)—messed up your mommy.

THOMAS. This is *monstrous*!

DOREEN. (*Rising from table, make-up completed.*) And that's putting it mildly!

BEVERLY. Here's your costume. (*Business of helping DOREEN into her dress.*)

THOMAS. That's *it*?

DOREEN. *What's* it, darling?

THOMAS. That's the *costume* you're going to wear in the next act?

BEVERLY. What's wrong with it?

THOMAS. (*The eyes of a fiend glowing in his face.*) Oh, it's fine, just fine. But it needs *accessories*! (*Steps to [unseen] area behind clothes rack, comes out with full-length coat.*) *Surely* you're going to wear your *mink* with it!

DOREEN. (*Pats him on the cheek.*) Thomas, my sweet, you *do* understand!

BEVERLY. (*Takes mink.*) Here, let me help you into it—

DOREEN Wait, I have to use the ladies room first. Be right back, darlings! (*Exits from room.*)

BEVERLY. She's taking it so bravely, the poor dear.

THOMAS. After hearing *her* news, telling her *our* revelations should be a breeze!

BEVERLY. See? There's always a silver lining to every situation—

WOLFGANG. (*Appears in doorway, a volcano just short of eruption.*) *Vhere* is she?!

BEVERLY. (*To THOMAS, completing her line.*)—but this isn't it.

WOLFGANG. (*Moving ominously into room.*) Vhere is dot *voman*?!

THOMAS. Now-now, Wolfgang, don't excite yourself. When you hear the explanation—

WOLFGANG. I von't *vait* for eggs-plon-ation! First I kill, *den* I listen!

BEVERLY. Stop dramatizing!

WOLFGANG. (*Shrugs.*) I am dramatist. How *else* should I act?

MEL. (*Pops into room.*) Has Doreen come offstage yet—*WOLFGANG*! (*Staggers back.*)

WOLFGANG. Zo! I find you at last! Dee man who *roo-wined* mine *play*!

MEL. (*A terrified peep.*) The audience *loves* it—! (*Backing out of room slowly.*) You should *hear* them chatting in the lobby—!

WOLFGANG. (*Advancing on him step-by-step.*) Dey is going to luff dee *zecond* act eefen *more*, vhen dee coortain rises on *your daad body*! (*Gives incoherent cry of rage, charges at MEL, who turns and runs, and the two of them go thundering off and out of view and earshot, MEL screaming all the way.*)

BEVERLY. This would make a marvelous murder mystery. Everybody has a motive to kill everybody else.

THOMAS. If that's another one of your silver linings, it needs work.

PAUL. (*Lurches into room, fingers flexed for strangulation.*) *Where* is she?!

BEVERLY. Look, Paul, if you want to murder Doreen, you'll have to get in line.

THOMAS. (*Slips behind PAUL, firmly closes dressing room door during:*) He won't have *time* to get in line, Bev. Because I'm going to murder him first!

PAUL. (*Menace turns to bewildered apprehension.*) Now, wait a minute, Tommy-boy! I know the noble thing is to defend your mother, but—?

THOMAS. (*Advancing upon him.*) I'm not going to kill you for what you *plan* to do to Doreen. I'm going to kill you for what you've already *done* to Doreen!

PAUL. (*Backing away.*) What? *What* have I done? Oh, sure, I sneezed during her big speech, but that was *her* fault!

BEVERLY. Do you *deny* you're the father of her child?!

PAUL. Her child? What child? You mean *Tommy*?

THOMAS. She means my baby brother!

BEVERLY. *Or* sister!

THOMAS. Whoever!

PAUL. Baby? What baby? When did *this* happen?

BEVERLY. *You* tell *us*! Paul, how *could* you do such a thing to Doreen!

PAUL. What the hell are you people *talking* about?!

THOMAS. As if you didn't *know,* you slimy rat!

BEVERLY. Wait, Tommy! Maybe he *doesn't* know!

THOMAS. After what *he* did to her?

BEVERLY. I mean maybe he didn't know he got *results*!

PAUL. Wait—are you saying—are you implying—are you telling me—that you think Doreen and I—?!

BEVERLY. (*To THOMAS.*) And *you* say *women* never finished their sentences!

PAUL. Hold it! It's not true! Not even slightly! I've hardly even held *hands* with the woman!

THOMAS. (*Now uncertain.*) Maybe you forgot—?

BEVERLY. Oh, now, *really,* Tommy!

PAUL. Listen—both of you—listen—if Doreen's having a baby, it certainly isn't *mine*!

THOMAS. There's no "if" *about* it! She *told* us, here, tonight, in this very room! Why do you think she's been out on the stage trying to make you sneeze your career to oblivion?!

PAUL. Is *that* why she's doing it?!

BEVERLY. Why *else*?!

PAUL. Well, she's barking up the wrong nose!

THOMAS. Paul, if *you* didn't get Mother pregnant, *who did*?

PAUL. For heaven's sake, Tommy, I'm not your mother's *sole* admirer!

THOMAS. What's *admiration* got to do with this?!

BEVERLY. Oh, Paul, and I was *so* certain you were actually in *love* with her!

PAUL. I *am* in love with her, damn it! Why else would I be backing this stupid *play*?! (*Realizes that he's blabbed too much.*) Oops. That slipped out.

BEVERLY. (*Gasps, points a finger accusingly at him.*) *Nunzio!*

THOMAS. *What?*

PAUL. (*Sinks into chair.*) It's just as well. I couldn't expect to keep the secret forever. Yes, I'm the guy who's supposed to be menacing Mel's kneecaps! I *had* to do it this way!

THOMAS. Why?

PAUL. Because—

BEVERLY. —you knew she'd be too proud to accept charity!

PAUL. So—

BEVERLY. —you used a phony identity to give money to Mel to produce this play!

PAUL. Hoping—

BEVERLY. —that being near to you again, Doreen's old feelings for you would be rekindled!

THOMAS. Paul, why didn't you *tell* me?!

PAUL. (*Considering all her preceding interruptions, shrugs, on:*) Why didn't *Beverly* tell you?!

BEVERLY. I didn't *know*!

PAUL. You coulda fooled *me*!

BEVERLY. I'm just a good guesser.

THOMAS. Paul, I owe you an apology. But who do I owe a punch in the nose?

BEVERLY. Yes, who *else* could be the father of Doreen's child?

MEL. (*Pops head into room.*) Where is that woman?! Why is she trying to *destroy* me?! What'd I ever do to *her*? (*Then he reacts to the stares of the trio, on:*) Why are you all looking at me?

WOLFGANG. (*O.S. from distance.*) *V*here is he?!

MEL. (*Stepping into room.*) Hide me! (*Takes quick look out doorway.*)

(*THOMAS, BEVERLY and PAUL simultaneously stare at MEL.*)

BEVERLY. Why should we hide you?

MEL. (*Crosses to BEVERLY.*) Because that Austrian lunatic is going to kill me.

BEVERLY. So?!

THOMAS. (*To BEVERLY.*) Wolfgang could save us the trouble of killing him *ourselves*.

MEL. In case you hadn't heard—it is *extremely* bad luck for the playwright to kill the producer on opening night.

THOMAS. Then I guess we'll *have* to do it ourselves!

BEVERLY. But that would leave my *brother-in-law* without a father.

THOMAS. Good point.

PAUL. (*Crosses over to MEL.*) You cad! (*Grabs fistful of Mel's shirtfront, going nose-to-nose with him growling in rage, one doubled up fist raised as if to strike, then gives up, releasing MEL, then exits.*)

MEL. (*Cowering in confusion and fear.*) What the hell's going on here? Has everyone gone crazy?

WOLFGANG. (*Off louder than before.*) I vill *kill* him!

MEL. (*Straightens up with terror and crosses to Thomas; then pleads.*) Please hide me. You can do whatever you want to me, but please hide me from that Bavarian Barbarian.

THOMAS. Whatever you say, *Dad.*

MEL. (*Totally confused.*) Dad? Sure, you can call me dad if you like—but save me!

BEVERLY. Okay, *Dad*! (*Grabs dress and wig from Doreen's costume rack and hands them to MEL.*) Put these on.

MEL. (*Looks at dress and wig.*) I wouldn't be caught *dead* in that outfit!

THOMAS. That's the *idea*, dumdum! Put them on! (*Crosses to door and looks out.*) If you want to hide from Wolfgang, I suggest you do it *fast!*

BEVERLY. There's no place else to hide, *Dad.* Your time's about up.

MEL. What choice do I have? (*Puts on wig and dress.*)

BEVERLY. Good. (*Drags MEL over to chair by make-up mirror.*) Now sit over here and act like you're putting on make-up.

MEL. I can't do this!

BEVERLY. Sit down. Think about the child.

MEL. (*Starts to sit down.*) Sure. I'll do it for the child. (*Springs out of seat.*) *What* child?

THOMAS. No time! Here comes Wolfgang. (*BEVERLY pushes MEL back into his seat and hands him make-up brush, THOMAS reaches over, picks up Fluffy and tosses it to BEVERLY, who places it on Mel's lap just as WOLFGANG enters.*)

WOLFGANG. (*Determinedly.*) Vhere *is* dat man?

BEVERLY. (*Brushing the wig on MEL as MEL puts on make-up.*) I really think you need to use just a little bit more powder.

WOLFGANG. (*Moving toward MEL.*) Zo *dere* is dat voman! (*To THOMAS.*) Say *auf wiedersehen* to your mama. If I can't kill dat vorthless prodoocer, *den* I kill his—(*Spots Fluffy.*) Oh, a poochee! It reminds uf a leetle doggee I hat vhen I vas a boy. (*Gets maudlin and weepy.*) I miss my leetle veener schnitzel doggee. Hiz name vas Vilhelm. He got run over by a pickle truck.

THOMAS. (*Crosses over to WOLFGANG.*) And think how sad Fluffy would feel if anything happened to Doreen. You couldn't do that to this poor little puppy, could you?

WOLFGANG. (*Still in tears.*) I can't do dis to der doggee. (*Kisses MEL on cheek.*) You joost do der best you can out dere. I go find my zeat. (*Slowly, sadly exits.*)

THOMAS. (*Waits a beat or two after WOLFGANG has left, then rushes to door and looks out.*) He's gone!

BEVERLY. Mel, you'd better keep the costume on in case Wolfgang spots you.

MEL. (*Stands and turns around.*) Good idea! But what if he *recognizes* the dress? I'm seated *next* to him out front!

BEVERLY. Just say, "My dear. The designer *promised* me that this was a one-of-a-kind."

MEL. (*Handing BEVERLY Fluffy.*) I want to thank you for saving my hide.

THOMAS. Don't thank us too soon, *Dad.* You're not out of the woods yet. You still have to deal with—

MEL. —Nunzio. *Right!* (*Takes quick look at self in mirror.*) Great costume!

BEVERLY. But you don't have to worry about—

MEL. —Doreen. I know she'll come through for me. She's a great gal.

THOMAS. I'm glad you think so. We've got to have a *long* talk.

MEL. (*Adjusting wig and costume.*) After the show. I've got to get to my seat. The second act should be starting soon. Where's Doreen?

BEVERLY. She's powdering her nose.

MEL. Right. (*Exiting as DOREEN enters.*) Doreen, see you after the show.

DOREEN. Who was that? A fan after my autograph?

BEVERLY. That was Mel.

DOREEN. Really? I never knew. The strain must have gotten to him. *Poor* man!

THOMAS. No. That was just a disguise. *Wolfgang Ferris* was hunting for him, so we gave him a wig and dress to hide out in.

DOREEN. *Wolfgang's* been back here?

BEVERLY. In the flesh.

DOREEN. Oh, dear! What did he think of the first act?

THOMAS. What do *you* think? You're lucky you were in the bathroom. He had *murder* in his eyes. Either *you* or *Mel*.

BEVERLY. So we dressed Mel as you and—well— Fluffy here saved your life—or Mel's.

DOREEN. *(Takes Fluffy from BEVERLY.)* I *knew* it. Just like Fluffy's hero Lassie. *(Petting Fluffy.)* Momma's good little boy.

BEVERLY. *(To THOMAS.)* You'd better tell her about Paul before she ruins the *second* act.

DOREEN. Tell me *what*? What about Paul?

THOMAS. *(Leads DOREEN to sofa.)* You'd better sit down. Normally I'd wait until after the show, but—

DOREEN. Don't tell me. That masher's *already* married?!

THOMAS. No, nothing like that. Paul's not the father. After you left, we spoke with him and we're positive he's *not* the father.

DOREEN. It had to be Paul. If not Paul, then who? I don't let *that* many sex-crazed men into my apartment.

BEVERLY. *(Sits beside DOREEN.)* He says it *couldn't* have been.

DOREEN. Well, it's *got* to be *somebody*!

BEVERLY. (*Very reluctant.*) Don't you think we could tell you after the show?

DOREEN. You think I could go out *there* with this on my mind? I won't go on until I know. I'm a professional. I can take it. *Who's* the father?

THOMAS. We figure it has to be—*Mel!*

(*DOREEN smiles briefly then faints.*)

THOMAS. (*Gently rubbing Doreen's hand.*) Mother. Mother. (*To BEVERLY.*) I knew we shouldn't have told her.

DOREEN. (*Comes to and acts like nothing has happened.*) Well, it's about time for the second act to start. (*Stands.*) I *am* a professional! And when I get through with the second act of this play *Melvin* won't be able to produce a *dog fight.* I *guarantee* that this play will end faster than an ice cube in the Sahara Desert. The man is *toast!*

THOMAS. Calm down, Mother. Remember, you're talking about my future father. (*Just then MEL comes in, still in costume.*)

THOMAS. Mel!

BEVERLY. Mel!

MEL. (*Unsuspecting.*) Beverly, do you happen to have a hair pin to help keep the wig from shifting?

DOREEN. Melvin, *darling,* before I go on stage, may I have a word with you in the hallway?

MEL. Certainly, Doreen. I *always* have time for you.

DOREEN. (*Puts arm around MEL and starts to head out.*) See you kids after the show.

(DOREEN and MEL exit together, closing door as they do. After a beat there is a the sound of a SLAP that could be heard around the world. BEVERLY and THOMAS wince.)

MEL. *(Re-enters holding side of face.)* She *hit* me! I don't get it! What did I do to deserve *that?*

BEVERLY. *(Scornfully.)* Do you deny Doreen is carrying your *child?!*

MEL. *(Stares at her for two beats, in bewilderment, then says:) Fluffy?!*

THOMAS. *(Furious.)* Your *other* child!

BEVERLY. *(Patiently.)* Thomas—

THOMAS. *(Recovering.)* I mean *the* other child—*an* other child—your child and Doreen's!

MEL. *(At sea.)* All *I* saw was *Fluffy*—

BEVERLY. We are *speaking* about Doreen's *pregnancy!*

MEL. What?! *(Semi-collapse into chair.)* She can't be pregnant!

THOMAS. Why not?

MEL. There's a *morals* clause in her contract!

BEVERLY. Aren't you a little bit *late* in *remembering* that?

MEL. *(It's sinking in now.)* Wait a minute—*(Will stand, slowly, during:)* You think that *I*—that *she* and—that I—that she—that we—?!

THOMAS. Will you stop conjugating pronouns?!

BEVERLY. You don't conjugate pronouns, you conjugate verbs.

THOMAS. Well, those two did *something* conjugal!

MEL. I never! I swear! Why would I? What would people say?! What would *Sophie* say?!

BEVERLY. Who's Sophie?

MEL. My fiancee!

THOMAS. "Fiancee"?! You're going to marry somebody *else*?

MEL. I'm not married. How can I marry someone else?

BEVERLY. He means beside Doreen!

MEL. But I'm not *married* to Doreen!

THOMAS. (*About to kill.*) And you don't even *plan* to be, you rotten cad?!

MEL. (*Very uneasy, but logical.*) Not—not particularly. I mean, how would it look to Sophie?

BEVERLY. But what about the *baby*?

MEL. (*Stands tall.*) Do I look like the kind of monster who'd get a lady pregnant out of wedlock?!

THOMAS. (*Grudgingly.*) Well, not in *that* outfit!

BEVERLY. Wait a minute—if *you* didn't get Doreen pregnant, and *Paul* didn't get Doreen pregnant, who else *is* there that could be responsible?

(*There is a pause, as all think hard; Then THOMAS and MEL go wide-eyed, turn to one another, and reach a unified conclusion:*)

THOMAS/MEL. *Wolfgang!*

BEVERLY. All the way from *Bavaria*?!

MEL. He *can* afford *air*fare—

THOMAS. Are you saying my new baby brother is Bavarian?

MEL. Blame it on the Concorde.

BEVERLY. But, how could Doreen *do* such a thing?

THOMAS. It's not as though it was her *idea*, Bev. I mean she doesn't seem very certain who the proud father *is*, even!

(PAUL enters, now relatively sneezeless and calm, goes right to MEL. takes his hands.)

PAUL. I want you to know—I *forgive* you, darling!

THOMAS. (*To BEVERLY*.) Well, now we're *sure* neither one of *them* is the father!

MEL. Forgive me for *what*, Paul?

PAUL. (*Scanning MEL a bit more closely*.) Do you know—you sound like *Mel*. You even *look* like Mel— (*Drops hands, takes backstep*.) Holy Toledo, you *are* Mel! What have you done with Doreen?

MEL. *Nothing*, but nobody will *believe* me!

BEVERLY. Paul means, where *is* she, Mel?

PAUL. (*Misinterpreting*.) Oh, no! She's been taken ill! And Mel's going on in her place?! I thought *sneezing* onstage was bad. Now I'm probably going to *throw up*!

THOMAS. Mel is not taking over for Doreen, Paul.

PAUL. Then why is he *dressed* like that?

BEVERLY. To hide from *Nunzio*!

THOMAS. *And* Wolfgang.

PAUL. But, didn't you *tell* him about Nunzio?

BEVERLY. We really haven't had much *chance*, Paul, what with various rages and accusations and—

MEL. What about Nunzio?

THOMAS. *Paul* is Nunzio!

MEL. (*Screams of terror*.) It's a trap! You all set me up, and I fell for it! (*Clutches PAUL by the lapels*.) One request! One *last* request?! After you kill me, dress me in my *own* clothes again? It's going to be tough *enough* on Sophie without her thinking I was a cross-dresser!

PAUL. Mel, I am *not* going to *kill* you!

MEL. (*Backstep.*) Torture! *That's* your plan! Oh, *please* don't! I'd *much* rather be killed.

BEVERLY. Mel, stop whimpering and *listen,* we can clear this up in just a moment—!

THOMAS. (*Intrigued.*) Even who got Mother pregnant?

BEVERLY. Okay, *two* moments! Him first, her later.

PAUL. We don't have *time* to clear things up *now!* The *curtain's* going up any minute—

MEL. Well, get *out* there! We can't start the second act with Doreen doing a *monologue!*

BEVERLY. And carrying *Fluffy!*

THOMAS. (*Looks out through door.*) The curtain *is* up!

BEVERLY. Is Doreen onstage?

THOMAS. Yeah, but I can't hear what she's ad-libbing to Fluffy.

PAUL. Yipe! Let me *out* of here! (*Bolts from room.*)

MEL. Now what's all this about Paul being Nunzio?

PAUL. (*Bolts back into room.*) *I* can't go onstage while she's holding that *dog!* I used up all my nasal spray during intermission!

THOMAS. It's a *fake* dog, Paul, with fake *fur,* remember?!

PAUL. Oh, of course, how stupid of me! (*Bolts out again, and we hear him get onstage with:*) "Ah, so *there* you are, dear lady! And your—um—lovely little *dog,* too. How nice."

MEL. (*Shuts door to cut off sound.*) Now, will somebody *please* tell me about Paul being Nunzio?

BEVERLY. Well, it's this way, Mel—

(Door opens and WOLFGANG storms in.)

WOLFGANG. Vhy is der a *dog* in mein play? *(Reacts to MEL.)* Und how did you get offen der *stage* so fast? *(Looks closer.)* Vait! *Du bist nicht* Doreen! *Du bist Mel!* *(Clutches MEL by upper arms.)* Vhy ist da doggie *der* und dis dress *here*? *(Pulls MEL to his feet.)* Vhy, I ask you?

MEL. Vhich qvestion—*(Corrects himself.)* *Which question* should I answer first?

WOLFGANG. *Eeder* one!

MEL. I have no idea.

WOLFGANG. Vhich one did you answer?

MEL. The doggie one.

BEVERLY. *I* can answer that one, Wolfgang. We decided to have Doreen carry Fluffy onstage in memory of your own *dead* doggie that got hit by the pickle truck!

THOMAS. It's sort of an *engagement* present!

WOLFGANG. But—I'm not engaged—?!

BEVERLY. But you're *going* to be.

THOMAS. Or I may have to murder you.

BEVERLY. If Paul doesn't murder him first.

MEL. And *Doreen* might like a crack at him herself!

WOLFGANG. *(Bewildered, sinks into chair.)* Murder me? All uff you?

BEVERLY. Well, one at a time.

WOLFGANG. *(Misunderstanding their motives.)* But I thought it vuz a *nize* leetle play!

MEL. Wolfgang, they are not murdering you because of your *play*!

THOMAS. Though it's an *idea*—

WOLFGANG. (*Stands.*) But *I* didn't put in der schneezing, *I* didn't put in der doggie, I didn't even *write* most of vhat dey're doing (*Closer to "doo-ink."*) on dot stage out der!

BEVERLY. But it's your *fault* they're doing it! After what you did to Doreen—!

WOLFGANG. Vhat? *Vhat?* VHAT?

MEL. Don't pretend you didn't hear her!

WOLFGANG. Not vhat-are-you-saying, vhat-did-I-*do*?!

THOMAS. Do you deny that you are the father of the child Doreen is carrying?!

WOLFGANG. (*Same wavelength as MEL earlier.*) *Fluffy*?!

BEVERLY. Wolfgang, Doreen is *pregnant*!

WOLFGANG. (*Uncertainly.*) Prag-nunt—?

THOMAS. What is it in Bavarian?

MEL. I think the word is "*schwunner*" [Pronounced "SHVUN-er]!

WOLFGANG. (*Drops into chair again.*) *Ach, du lieber*!

MEL. (*Defensively.*) Don't looken-*Sie* at *mir*, Wolfgang. If anyone's a "lieber" around here, it's *Du*!

THOMAS. You mean the *baby* is due!

WOLFGANG. (*At sea.*) Ich bin ein *baby*?

BEVERLY. Hey, why don't we start all over from the beginning?

THOMAS. 'Cause we don't know where we began!

MEL. I'd *really* like to know about this *Nunzio* situation. At least, my *knees* would.

WOLFGANG. Nunzio? Knees?

BEVERLY. Maybe this all began back in Bavaria!

THOMAS. Well, it's a *start*—

(Then ALL pause as DOREEN races into run with Fluffy in her arms; she places the dog on the dressing table, turns and starts out again, but pauses for:)

THOMAS. Mother, *wait*!

DOREEN. Can't! I have to get back onstage before Paul runs out of ad-libs!

WOLFGANG. Ad-libs?! In *mein* play?!

DOREEN. We had to do *something* to account for our actions! Right now it's beginning to look as if the *dog* is the murderer! Comb his fur, will you, Beverly? I want him to look his best in the final scene!

(DOREEN dashes out, MEL screams, WOLFGANG faints, THOMAS turns to BEVERLY, and:)

THOMAS. Well, if this show's a *hit*, I hope they've written everything *down*!

BLACKOUT

END ACT II
Scene 1

ACT II

Scene 2

Doreen's dressing room, about half an hour later. BEVERLY is on loveseat, her head back, her eyes closed, not sleeping, but looking rested. THOMAS is slumped in chair at dressing table. Flyffy is gon again.

THOMAS. I need a cigarette.

BEVERLY. (*Without opening eyes.*) You don't smoke.

THOMAS. I figure it's time to start.

BEVERLY. Then do it outside. I don't want to pollute the baby.

THOMAS. Are you *sure* about the baby?

BEVERLY. Well, it can't be a *gerbil*.

THOMAS. I mean the test results.

BEVERLY. They'll call, they'll call. Why don't you just relax!

THOMAS. I can't believe they'll call at *this* time of night.

BEVERLY. Yes they will. My doctor *knows* I keep weird hours. No one would *dare* call a theater person in the *morning*.

(A ROAR of audience laughter, off.)

THOMAS. There they go *again!*

BEVERLY. Take it easy, Tommy. Neil Simon would *kill* for laughs like that!

THOMAS. In a *drama*? Wolfgang's script sounds like it's been put through a meat-grinder!

BEVERLY. It's not *that* bad. Every so often I hear a line from the *original* script.

THOMAS. That's probably the only reason he hasn't blown his brains out. What gets me is that the audience seems to be *enjoying* the show, despite the fact that it's certainly not the show they paid to *see*.

BEVERLY. Tommy, honey, they don't *know* what the show's supposed to be about. They paid to see *Doreen* in her triumphant debut on the Broadway stage, and that's what they're getting.

THOMAS. They may get a *bonus*. If Wolfgang steps onstage and *shoots* her at the curtain call, they'll get Doreen's *farewell* performance at the same time!

BEVERLY. Now, now, he's surely not taking it *that* hard!

(But then WOLFGANG lurches into the room from the corridor, a broken man, sobbing his heart out; BEVERLY finally opens her eyes, sees him, and springs up from the loveseat just before he collapses onto it.)

WOLFGANG. (*Between sobs and sniffles.*) It's a nightmare. A nightmare! No. No it's not. From a nightmare I could *vake up*! People are laughing so hard the *chandeliers* are dancing!

THOMAS. (*Consolingly.*) Maybe you'll have another *Phantom of the Opera*, Wolfie.

BEVERLY. Don't give him ideas. You know how the Phantom behaved toward leading ladies.

(DOREEN rushes into the room, thrusts Fluffy into BEVERLY's hands.)

DOREEN. Here, take him. Paul and I finally worked the dog out of the plot! I've got to get back!

WOLFGANG. Vait! (*When she pauses short of exit:*) *Vun* thing explain to me, please!

DOREEN. Okay, but make it quick!

WOLFGANG. Vhy are you doing *Paul's* lines and *Paul* is doing *yours*?!

DOREEN. Paul *forgot* a line, earlier, and when I tried to back-feed it to him, he replied with *my* next line, so *I* had to respond with *his*, and we haven't figured a way *out* of it yet.

WOLFGANG. But you're both the wrong *sexes*!

THOMAS. Huh? What has gender got to do with it?

WOLFGANG. (*Almost whimpering.*) Yust before I came backstage to die, Doreen accused Paul of having an illegal *hysterectomy*, and then *he* accused *her* of needing a *shave*!

DOREEN. (*Quite at ease.*) Oh, don't worry about that. Paul and I covered matters beautifully!

WOLFGANG. (*Comes to his feet.*) In the name of heaven, *how*?

DOREEN. We came up with a quick "fix" in the dialogue, and now the audience thinks we're a pair of *transvestites*! (*WOLFGANG, speechless, lets his mouth gape, chin dropping to chest, as DOREEN looks toward BEVERLY and THOMAS and adds:*) Cute, huh? (*She exits.*)

WOLFGANG. (*Finds his voice, even if he can't find actual words:*) AAAAAAAAAAAAHHH! (*Covers his face with both hands, drops onto loveseat, echoes:*) AAAH!—AAAH!—AAAH!

THOMAS. I think he's getting hysterical.

BEVERLY. *Getting* hysterical?!

(*MEL enters, still wigged and gowned.*)

MEL. I heard screaming. I thought the critics finally cornered Doreen.

BEVERLY. That was Wolfgang. He just found out that Doreen and Paul have changed their characters into transvestites.

MEL. (*Hands on hips.*) Where did they get a stupid idea like *that*—? (*When the twosome just stares at him, he looks down at his own outfit, reacts.*) Oh, come *on*, now, you're—surely not trying to fix the blame on *me*?

(Another ROAR of audience laughter, off.)

THOMAS. I'm not sure "blame" is the word. The audience is having the time of their lives.

WOLFGANG. (*Comes to his feet.*) I've got to get *out* there! If only I could stop sobbing! If they see me in *tears*, they're gonna *know* something's wrong!

BEVERLY. Why not take *Mel* with you?

MEL. What good would *that* do?

BEVERLY. If they think *you're* his date for the evening, it could *explain* why he looks so unhappy!

WOLFGANG. (*Shrugs.*) It's as good a plan as any! (*Links arms with MEL.*) Come on, *liebchen*! (*They exit.*)

BEVERLY. Poor *Wolfgang*! His *writing* career is finished!

THOMAS. Poor *Mother*! Her *acting* career is over! (*Sudden thought.*) I'm going to need to get a better job! (*Crosses over to loveseat and sits dejectedly.*) As a matter of fact, I may need to get *three* jobs.

BEVERLY. What are you talking about?

THOMAS. Don't you see? Wolfgang won't even be able to get a job writing *want ads*—and I know Mother will *never* be able to work again. Talk about burning your bridges! They *blew 'em up*!

BEVERLY. What does that have to do with you having to get *three* jobs?

THOMAS. After Wolfgang marries Mother, and *their* baby is born and *our* baby is born, our family will consist of *six*. Wolfgang and Mother won't be able to get work. It'll all be on *my* shoulders.

BEVERLY. (*Comforting him.*) Someone else can help.

THOMAS. What kind of work can *babies* get?

BEVERLY. No, me, you dunderhead!

THOMAS. Thanks, but with *six* mouths to feed, we won't be able to *afford* child care.

BEVERLY. What about Doreen?

THOMAS. I don't think a woman Doreen's *age* will be able to keep up with two babies. No, you're going to have to stay home while I work *three* jobs.

BEVERLY. But *our* child will never get to see his *father*.

THOMAS. I'll take a day off when *he* and my *half-brother* graduate from high school.

BEVERLY. But, when will I see you?

THOMAS. (*Sadly.*) You can sit next to me at graduation.

BEVERLY. (*Embracing.*) Oh, Thomas!

(*They kiss, then break.*)

THOMAS. (*Thoughtfully.*) I can't get used to the idea of calling Wolfgang Papa.

BEVERLY. Oh dear, I can't stand the suspense any longer. I'm going to call my *doctor*! Those test results *must* be in by now! I can't stand all this continued lying to Doreen!

THOMAS. This could be the *perfect* time to break the news, come to think of it.

BEVERLY. In what way?

THOMAS. Just before Wolfgang's fingers encircle Doreen's throat, we can say, "*Surely* you wouldn't lay violent hands on a *grandmother*?!

BEVERLY. Tommy, when Doreen hears "grandmother," her *own* hands may encircle her throat!

(Another ROAR of laughter from the audience, off.)

THOMAS. I'm worried about Mel going out front in drag. He's too old to be Wolfgang's date!

BEVERLY. So he'll pass Mel off as his Aunt Hilga! *(Starts for phone.)* I'm going to make that call.

THOMAS. Wolfgang's in too much of a daze to think that fast. What if he calls his date "Mel"?

BEVERLY. He'd better not. He's seated right next to the reviewer for the Times! But the laughing's so loud, maybe nobody'll overhear.

THOMAS. And if they *do*?

BEVERLY. Wolfgang will hop on the first plane back to Bavaria! Which means your half-brother—

THOMAS. —or *sister*—

BEVERLY. —won't have a papa!

THOMAS. Considering everything *else* going on tonight, that all seems a *minor* problem! *(Suddenly looks at wristwatch.)* Say, I'm not positive, but isn't it getting pretty close to the final *curtain* of the show?

BEVERLY. With all the *changes*, for all we know, the second act could run for hours. We could have ourselves another *Nicholas Nickleby*.

THOMAS. I'd better check. (*Crosses to entrance followed by roar of audience LAUGHTER.*) Well the audience is *still* out there. They haven't left.

BEVERLY. (*Crossing to THOMAS.*) Probably the same morbid *fascination* as watching a *train* wreck, but in this case, watching everyone associated with this production wrecking their *careers*.

THOMAS. Does that mean I need to *change* my name to get a decent job?

BEVERLY. You could always take *Wolfgang's*.

THOMAS. Ferris? I don't *think* so! Besides his name's connected to *this* production.

BEVERLY. You're right.

(*Huge LAUGHTER from audience followed by thunderous APPLAUSE, off.*)

THOMAS. Sounds like that's *it*! (*Both listen carefully.*) Should be taking curtain calls about—

(*Long roll of APPLAUSE followed by "bravos!", off.*)

THOMAS. I'll be *damned*, they seem to *like* it.

(*Another wave of APPLAUSE with "bravos" mixed in, off.*)

BEVERLY. (*Excitedly.*) They *love* it! (*They embrace.*)

(Final wave of APPLAUSE and "bravos!", off.)

THOMAS. *(Tickled at audience reaction.)* I *can't* believe it. I expected the exit of the cast from the stage to resemble *lemmings* heading to the sea. *(Crossing to C.S.)* But, from the audience reaction, I'd say that this *show's* a *hit!*

BEVERLY. *(Crossing to THOMAS.)* But with all the *changes* in lines and blocking, can it ever be *repeated*?

THOMAS. Got me. *(Enthusiastically.)* But it means that Mother's career's *not* ruined. Wolfgang's career *isn't* ruined. That means *I* don't have to get *three* jobs and I can spend time with my *family. Our* child. My half-brother or sister. My *wife!* *(They embrace again.)*

DOREEN. *(Entering victoriously into room with individual roses in arms.)* Doreen's return to the stage was a *triumph!* My audience *loved* me. *(Suddenly sees THOMAS and BEVERLY embraced.)* *What* in the world is going on here?

THOMAS. *(Surprised.)* Uh—we were—just—uh— *(Breaks away.)*

BEVERLY. —*taken* by the *excitement* of your performance.

DOREEN. Oh. *(Satisfied, goes back to herself.)* It was just like the *old* days. It was *magic* on stage.

THOMAS. Yeah, like pulling a *rabbit* out of a hat.

BEVERLY. *(Noticing roses.)* What *pretty* flowers!

DOREEN. *(Beaming.)* The stage was *strewn* with them. My *adoring* fans, you know. And *Fluffy* was just like a veteran on stage. Not a *touch* of stage fright! And his *first* play! Of course, he *was* with his mama. *(Picks up Fluffy.)* *Mama* is *so* proud of you!

BEVERLY. (*Whispering to THOMAS.*) I think we need to tell her about us.

THOMAS. But why should I *spoil* her upbeat mood?

BEVERLY. I think we need to get the whole thing out into the open. I want *everyone* to know. We've got nothing to be ashamed about.

DOREEN. (*Just catching end of Beverly's line.*) Ashamed of *what*?

THOMAS. We're just *ashamed* that we didn't get you flowers ourselves. (*Hard stare from BEVERLY.*) *Okay*! Mother, Beverly and I have something *else* to tell you. You see—

(*Suddenly there is a KNOCK and PAUL, all smiles, comes through the door.*)

DOREEN. (*Going to PAUL immediately.*) And here is my sweet, sweet, leading man! (*Puts huge hug on PAUL, which takes him completely off guard.*) It was *s o* wonderful, darling. We were *spectacular* on stage, weren't we? (*Realizing that Fluffy is in hug.*) Beverly, dear, be a doll and hold Fluffy, please.

BEVERLY. Sure. (*Crosses to DOREEN and takes Fluffy.*) Let me take those flowers and put them into some water. (*Takes flowers.*)

(*During following BEVERLY takes fake flowers out of vase and puts "real" flowers into vase:*)

DOREEN. (*Holding Paul's hand.*) Paul, *darling*, it was *so* good to be with you out there on stage. It was *just* like the good ol' days, when we used to act together on stage.

But *this* time, especially in the second act, it was *special*. It was *fun*! The audience *loved* us, didn't they?

PAUL. (*Genuinely touched*.) It *was* fun wasn't it? It was *musical*. It was *lyrical*. It was *love!*

DOREEN. Paul, *darling*, let's not get carried away! (*Breaks away and crosses to in front of loveseat*.) We had something out on *stage*—something *special*. But, it was just a play.

PAUL. (*Crosses to her*.) Doreen, (*Grabs her hand*.) it *wasn't* the play. This play was a *disaster* from the first line to the final curtain.

DOREEN. What are you *saying*? You heard the audience reaction. They *loved* us. The play was a hit! *Three* standing ovations and *three* curtain calls!

PAUL. We did everything possible to *demolish* this play. We couldn't have cut it up more if we'd taken a *chain saw* to it. (*Eases DOREEN and self onto loveseat*.) But try as hard as we could, we couldn't ruin the *love* that existed on stage between the *two* of us.

DOREEN. *What* love? (*In denial*.) It was *just* the play.

PAUL. (*Firmly*.) Doreen, you're wrong. *I love you!* I've loved you for *years*. I was just afraid to let you know. That's why *I* financed this show.

DOREEN. (*Surprised*.) *You*? But I thought—

PAUL. I'm *Nunzio*.

THOMAS. He is!

DOREEN. (*Amazed*.) *You* knew?

BEVERLY. We just found out tonight.

PAUL. I made Mel hire *both* of us, so I could be on stage with *you* again.

BEVERLY. Wait a *minute*! *Why* was Mel going around in such fear of losing his kneecaps?

PAUL. He just found out *tonight* that I was Nunzio. Doreen, I *didn't* care if this show was a hit *or* a flop, as long as *I* was onstage with *you. I* love you and want *you* to be my co-star on and off stage.

DOREEN. (*Almost giddy.*) I had *no* idea you felt this way, Paul. I'm *overwhelmed.* (*Suddenly she remembers the pregnancy.*) Paul, I have a *confession* to make. *I'm*—uh—

PAUL. *Pregnant.* I know. *I don't care.*

THOMAS. But what about *Wolfgang*?

PAUL. (*Incredulously.*) *Wolfgang*!

DOREEN. (*Just as surprised.*) *Wolfgang*! (*Faints.*)

PAUL. *He's* the father? (*To DOREEN.*) How *could* you? (*Stands.*) I'll *kill* him! (*DOREEN unfaints.*)

DOREEN. Paul, I cannot permit your killing the father of my child. (*Beat.*) Let *me* do it!

THOMAS. Before you do, Beverly and I have something to *tell* you.

DOREEN. Oh, all right, all right, what *is* it that you find so *urgent,* my dears?

THOMAS. Well, it's this way, dear. Beverly and I—

BEVERLY. Wait! Tommy, let me make that phone call first. Then we can lay *everything* on her in one fell swoop, you know what I mean?

THOMAS. You're probably right. Go ahead and call.

PAUL. Why don't you call from *my* dressing room, Beverly, it's going to get crowded in here.

BEVERLY. Good idea, Paul. Thanks. (*Exits to corridor.*)

DOREEN. Thomas, you two have succeeded in getting me quite *maddeningly* curious! What in the *world* can be so mysterious and so important and—?!

THOMAS. It'll keep, darling. I'd rather wait for Beverly so we can tell you *together*.

PAUL. (*Getting an inkling.*) Thomas, about this sudden *togetherness* of you and Beverly—

THOMAS. Well, actually, Paul, it isn't *sudden* at *all*.

PAUL. (*Gets it.*) Oh, I think I begin to see—

DOREEN. Well, *I* don't. Must be all the opening-night excitement. My brain's not functioning. Can't you even give me a *hint* about what you're keeping from me—?

PAUL. If it's what I think it is, I agree with your son: Wait for Beverly to come back.

DOREEN. But honestly, Paul—!

(*DOREEN stops as MEL enters from corridor, his eyes wide, his face incredulous.*)

THOMAS. Mel, what *is* it? You look like Pierre Curie discovering radium!

PAUL. Make that *Marie* Curie.

MEL. I have the most marvelous news. We're a hit! At least, with the *New York Times*!

DOREEN. A hit?

THOMAS. But only in the Times?

MEL. *Maybe* the other papers. The Times is the only one I know about.

PAUL. But it's the one that *counts*!

DOREEN. How did you find *out*, Mel?

PAUL. Yes, the play critics in this town are downright *zipper*-lipped until they write their reviews!

MEL. (*Now the undisputed center of rapt attention.*) I peeked at his notebook, and couldn't hold off *saying* something to him.

THOMAS. What did you *say*?

MEL. I said, "What's an existentialist allegory?" And *he* said, "This *play*, of course!" and like a man showing off his insight and psychological know-how, he started *babbling* about the *hidden meaning* of the play, probably thinking I was some simple-minded first-nighter.

DOREEN. Wait! Hold on! "Existentialist allegory"?

PAUL. *What* "hidden meaning," for Pete's sake?!

MEL. He said the first act represented Snow White grown to maturity in the modern world!

THOMAS. Where did he get a silly notion like that?

MEL. He figured *Paul* represented the last surviving dwarf: *Sneezy!*

DOREEN. Do you know—it almost makes *sense!*

THOMAS. But that's crazy!

MEL. It gets crazier: In the *second* act, Snow White reveals that she is actually Dorothy Gale!

PAUL. Who's Dorothy Gale?

DOREEN. You don't mean the little girl in *The Wizard of Oz*?!

MEL. What *else* could he think, with you playing most of the act toting *Toto!*

THOMAS. It *still* doesn't make sense to me! I mean, Doreen and Paul *reversed* roles in the last act!

MEL. He took that into consideration. He said how *brilliant* of the playwright to realize that Dorothy was actually a *boy*, all along, and that her *aunt* was really her *uncle*, and—

PAUL. Hold it! You mean, after all my years in the theatre, I'm playing *Auntie Em*?!

MEL. What do *you* care?! That man is recommending the play for a *Pulitzer Prize!*

THOMAS. It's a damned good thing he didn't know "Boy Dorothy" was *pregnant!*

DOREEN. Oh, dear! In all the excitement, I *forgot* about that! Paul—darling—what in the *world* are we going to *do*? *I* don't want to marry *Wolfgang!*

PAUL. And you're not *going* to! (*WOLFGANG, starry-eyed and dazed, holding his right hand up before his face, palm inward, and not taking his eyes off it, enters during:*) When you have the baby, I intend to *adopt* it, and we'll raise it as our *own*, and leave Wolfgang entirely out of the picture. We won't even ask him for child-support!

WOLFGANG. (*This snaps him out of his happy daze.*) *Bless* you! *Both* of you! (*Holds hand toward them.*) Look at this hand! It was just shaken by the theatre critic of the *New York Times*! He told me that in his opinion I am the reigning playwright of this century! (*Clutches his hand against his chest with his other hand.*) I think I'll have it dipped in bronze.

DOREEN. I'll be happy to recommend a discreet foundry. (*Abruptly frowns.*) Say, where are all the *crowds* we've been anticipating? By *this* time, my dressing room is usually *crammed* with hordes of fans and well-wishers—?!

MEL. Omigosh! I forgot!

THOMAS. Forgot *what?*

MEL. When I was so worried about Nunzio and my knees, I hired an armed guard to stand outside the stage door and let *nobody* in!

PAUL. Well, no *wonder* it's so lonely back here!

DOREEN. Mel, for heaven's sake, go pay the man off and let everybody come in!

MEL. Yes, of course, at once, Doreen darling!

(But as he turns toward door, a jubilant BEVERLY pops in, and:)

BEVERLY. I'm pregnant!

MEL/PAUL/WOLFGANG. *(In terrified unison:)* I didn't do it!

THOMAS. Of course you didn't. *I* did! Darling! *(Takes BEVERLY into his arms.)*

DOREEN. Thomas, how could you *do* such a thing to Beverly?!

BEVERLY. It's all right. We're married! We were going to *surprise* you, Doreen!

DOREEN. Well, you certainly *s u c c e e d e d*! Congratulations, darlings! *(Rushes to hug them both.)*

PAUL. Yes, indeed, I think it's wonderful!

MEL. But when did you find out about the baby?

BEVERLY. It's the oddest thing: I gave up waiting to hear the test-results and phoned my doctor, and he said somebody had *already* phoned here with the results!

WOLFGANG. If so, then *who* took the *call*?

DOREEN. *(Realizes.)* *I* did! Of course! *(Rushes to Paul's arms.)* Darling, I'm *not* going to have a baby! *(Dubiously.)* Will you marry me *anyway*?

PAUL. Gee, I'm not sure I want to marry somebody's *grandmother*—!

OTHERS. *Paul*!

PAUL. Only kidding, only kidding! Can't a guy make a joke?

DOREEN. *(Holding him.)* Oh, darling, it'll be so wonderful! This play should run *forever*, if that Times reviewer and that *audience*-response are any indication.

There's nothing nicer in the theatre than having a happy marriage *and* co-starring in a humungous *hit*!

MEL. (*The start of consternation.*) Wait—hold on—I just realized—our super-duper *hit* is the show you two did *tonight*! Can you *remember* what you did?

DOREEN. Oh dear, I'm not *sure*—

PAUL. *I* spent the first half of the evening *sneezing,* that's all *I* remember!

THOMAS. This is terrible!

BEVERLY. If you can't remember *exactly* what you did on stage tonight, we're *doomed*!

DOREEN. The *stage manager*! He's on book for the entire performance! Surely he took *notes*?

MEL. I'm afraid the poor man got so *lost* trying to follow what *you* two were doing that he threw the script on the floor, stomped on it with both feet, and departed in tears!

PAUL. Oh hell! The hit of a lifetime and we don't know how to *repeat* it!

WOLFGANG. Does this mean no Pulitzer Prize?

THOMAS. Afraid so, Wolfie.

WOLFGANG. (*Sighs.*) Ah vell, it vas not to be! At least I'll have permanent happy *memories* of the show to solace me in mine old age! At least Aunt *Hilga* vill get to see it!

MEL. How can she *possibly*? We'll never be able to do it *again*!

WOLFGANG. Oh, I don't mean the *live* show. I mean vhen I play for her the *wideotape*!

DOREEN. *What* wideotape?

PAUL. Cameras aren't *allowed* inside a theatre during performances!

BEVERLY. Or *any* kind of *recording* devices!

MEL. It's *totally* against the rules!

THOMAS. Only a low-down sneaky *rat* would attempt to do such a thing!

WOLFGANG. I know. I had to *bribe* the lighting engineer to do it for me! I'm a no-good louse!

OTHERS. (*Arms wide for a wild embrace of the man.*) God bless you! (*They hug WOLFGANG en masse.*)

BEVERLY. Doreen! You and Paul can't just *stand around* like this! You've got to *get* that tape, take it home, and *study* the thing *all night,* so you can go on *tomorrow* night!

PAUL. Ye gods, she's right! We've got to get *out* of here!

DOREEN. Ah, but I *hate* to disappoint all my adoring *fans—*

THOMAS. The fans! Mel, you never called off that armed guard!

PAUL. Think of it—*hundreds* of people, *craving* our autographs in vain!

(*We abruptly hear MACHINE-PISTOL FIRE, off; after a pause:*)

DOREEN. Okay, then, *dozens* of people.

MEL. It's all right. I told him to fire the *first* burst over their heads as a *warning*!

THOMAS. Come on, Bev, let's *explain* matters to the man before he tries a *second* burst!

MEL. Why can't *I* do it?

BEVERLY. If you sidle up to the guard in *that* outfit, *you* may get that second burst! (*They rush out.*)

DOREEN. (*Spots that Star of David on dressing table, picks it up.*) What's *this*?

MEL. The star for your door.

DOREEN. But it's like the logo on kosher-food products! I'd feel like a *matzo ball*!

PAUL. Doreen, you *love* matzo balls!

DOREEN. Not enough to *be* one! (*Starts to put star down, then pauses for:*) On the other hand, I seem to recall that Times reviewer is Jewish. After his lovely review, the *least* I can do is accept this in his honor. Mel, this star will do *fine* on my door!

MEL. Sorry, Doreen, no can do. According to that very reviewer, you're *not* the star of the show!

PAUL. Then who *is*?

MEL. (*Shrugs.*) *Fluffy*!

OTHERS. *Fluffy*?!

MEL. He said he'd never *seen* a better-trained dog perform on a Broadway stage!

WOLFGANG. But Fluffy is *shtuffed*!

MEL. *He* doesn't know that. (*To threesome.*) *I* won't tell if *you* don't!

(*THOMAS and BEVERLY re-enter.*)

THOMAS. All taken care of.

BEVERLY. We explained matters to the guard and he unloaded and went home.

DOREEN. So where are my adoring fans?

THOMAS. Running for their lives down Shubert Alley!

BEVERLY. They didn't hang around for the second burst.

DOREEN. Oh well, there's always tomorrow night! And—(*Picks up Fluffy, takes him to dressing room door, closes it, and hangs him by his collar on a coat-hook there.*)—I *still* get a star on the door! (*OTHERS laugh appreciatively.*)

PAUL. (*Embraces DOREEN.*) And I get the love of my life at last!

THOMAS. And I get Beverly!

BEVERLY. And we get a baby!

MEL. And I get to keep my knees!

WOLFGANG. And *I* get a hot property worth *tons* of money!

DOREEN. Your slightly-revised *play*, you mean?

PAUL. "*Slightly*"?!

WOLFGANG. Bah! The play is nothing! I am shpeaking of an even *hotter* property!

OTHERS. *What* property?

WOLFGANG. (*Re-opens door, stands dramatically in doorway, and announces, with a villainous smile:*) Vhich vun of you vants to make the opening bid for mine *wideotape*—?!

(*And as OTHERS ad-lib cries of consternation and pleading ["Wolfie!"—"You wouldn't!" —"Wait!" — "Stop!" — etc.] and start for him, WOLFGANG, laughing merrily, gallops out of view, and as OTHERS take off after him, protesting frantically—.*)

THE CURTAIN FALLS

End of Show

PROPERTY PLOT

Make-up table and chair (set)
Loveseat (set)
Make-up, brushes, etc. (set)
Clothes rack (set)
Phone (set)
Dressing screen (set)
Fluffy (set)
Two portraits of Doreen (set)
Water and food bowls for Fluffy (set)
Picture of Lassie (set)
Plastic plants (set)
Bouquet of flowers for dressing table (set)
Old and worn telegrams (Beverly)
Feather duster (Beverly)
Wristwatch (Mel)
Six-inch Star of David (Mel)
Fur stole (Doreen)
Full-length fur coat (Doreen)
Wig and dress (Mel)
Wristwatch (Thomas)
Single roses (Doreen)